Instructions

CUT OUT THE COUPON OF YOUR
CHOICE ON THE WHITE DOTTED LINE.
MAKE THE COUPON A CARD BY
FOLDING IT AT THE WHITE SOLID
LINE. FILL OUT THE "TO" & "FROM"
AND THE REWARD (IF YOU ARE USING
A BLANK COUPON). AND VOILA, IT IS
READY TO BE GIFTED!

Redeem For

ONE TREAT OF YOUR CHOICE

VALID ON WEEKENDS & HOLIDAYS

Redeem For

HOST A SLEEPOVER

VALID ON WEEKENDS & HOLIDAYS

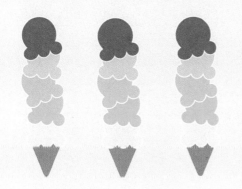

Redeem For

GO OUT FOR ICE CREAM

VALID WHENEVER!

Redeem For

PAJAMAS DAY

VALID ON WEEKENDS & HOLIDAYS

Redeem For

MINUTES OF EXTRA SCREEN TIME

VALID ON WEEKENDS & HOLIDAYS

TO:

FROM:

TO:

FROM:

TO:

FROM:

TO:

FROM:

TO:

FROM:

Redeem For

SKIP CHORES FOR
A DAY

VALID WHENEVER!

Redeem For

MOVIES AT
THE THEATERS
-WITH POPCORN-

VALID ON WEEKENDS & HOLIDAYS

Redeem For

BREAKFAST FOR
DINNER

VALID WHENEVER!

Redeem For

$ TO SPEND
AT A STORE

VALID WHENEVER!

Redeem For

STAY UP   HOUR
PAST BEDTIME

VALID ON WEEKENDS & HOLIDAYS

TO:

FROM:

TO:

FROM:

TO:

FROM:

TO:

FROM:

TO:

FROM:

Redeem For

DINNER AT A RESTAURANT OF YOUR CHOICE

VALID ON WEEKENDS & HOLIDAYS

Redeem For

DATE WITH DAD
YOUR CHOICE OF ACTIVITY

VALID ON WEEKENDS & HOLIDAYS

Redeem For

SKIP A VEGETABLE (OR ITEM OF YOUR CHOICE) FOR ONE MEAL

VALID WHENEVER!

Redeem For

GAME NIGHT
YOUR CHOICE OF GAME

VALID ON WEEKENDS & HOLIDAYS

Redeem For

EXTRA BEDTIME STORY(IES)

VALID WHENEVER!

TO:

FROM:

TO:

FROM:

TO:

FROM:

TO:

FROM:

TO:

FROM:

Redeem For

DATE WITH MOM
YOUR CHOICE OF ACTIVITY

VALID ON WEEKENDS & HOLIDAYS

Redeem For

FAMILY ACTIVITY
OF YOUR CHOICE

VALID ON WEEKENDS & HOLIDAYS

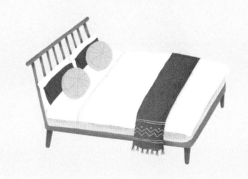

Redeem For

SLEEPOVER AT MOM
AND DAD'S ROOM

VALID ON WEEKENDS & HOLIDAYS

Redeem For

FAMILY
DANCE PARTY

VALID ON WEEKENDS & HOLIDAYS

Redeem For

ONE BREAKFAST
IN BED

VALID ON WEEKENDS & HOLIDAYS

TO:

FROM:

TO:

FROM:

TO:

FROM:

TO:

FROM:

TO:

FROM:

Redeem For

ONE TREAT OF YOUR CHOICE

VALID ON WEEKENDS & HOLIDAYS

Redeem For

HOST A SLEEPOVER

VALID ON WEEKENDS & HOLIDAYS

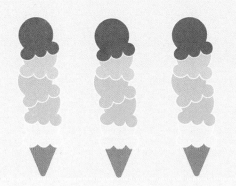

Redeem For

GO OUT FOR ICE CREAM

VALID WHENEVER!

Redeem For

PAJAMAS DAY

VALID ON WEEKENDS & HOLIDAYS

Redeem For

MINUTES OF EXTRA SCREEN TIME

VALID ON WEEKENDS & HOLIDAYS

TO:

FROM:

TO:

FROM:

TO:

FROM:

TO:

FROM:

TO:

FROM:

Redeem For

SKIP CHORES FOR
A DAY

Redeem For

MOVIES AT
THE THEATERS
-WITH POPCORN-

VALID ON WEEKENDS & HOLIDAYS

Redeem For

BREAKFAST FOR
DINNER

VALID WHENEVER!

Redeem For

$ TO SPEND
AT A STORE

VALID WHENEVER!

Redeem For

STAY UP HOUR
PAST BEDTIME

VALID ON WEEKENDS & HOLIDAYS

TO:

FROM:

TO:

FROM:

TO:

FROM:

TO:

FROM:

TO:

FROM:

Redeem For

DINNER AT A RESTAURANT OF YOUR CHOICE

VALID ON WEEKENDS & HOLIDAYS

Redeem For

DATE WITH DAD
YOUR CHOICE OF ACTIVITY

VALID ON WEEKENDS & HOLIDAYS

Redeem For

SKIP A VEGETABLE (OR ITEM OF YOUR CHOICE) FOR ONE MEAL

VALID WHENEVER!

Redeem For

GAME NIGHT
YOUR CHOICE OF GAME

VALID ON WEEKENDS & HOLIDAYS

Redeem For

EXTRA BEDTIME STORY(IES)

VALID WHENEVER!

TO:

FROM:

TO:

FROM:

TO:

FROM:

TO:

FROM:

TO:

FROM:

Redeem For

DATE WITH MOM
YOUR CHOICE OF ACTIVITY

VALID ON WEEKENDS & HOLIDAYS

Redeem For

FAMILY ACTIVITY
OF YOUR CHOICE

VALID ON WEEKENDS & HOLIDAYS

Redeem For

SLEEPOVER AT MOM
AND DAD'S ROOM

VALID ON WEEKENDS & HOLIDAYS

Redeem For

FAMILY
DANCE PARTY

VALID ON WEEKENDS & HOLIDAYS

Redeem For

ONE BREAKFAST
IN BED

VALID ON WEEKENDS & HOLIDAYS

TO:

FROM:

TO:

FROM:

TO:

FROM:

TO:

FROM:

TO:

FROM:

Redeem For

ONE TREAT OF YOUR CHOICE

VALID ON WEEKENDS & HOLIDAYS

Redeem For

HOST A SLEEPOVER

VALID ON WEEKENDS & HOLIDAYS

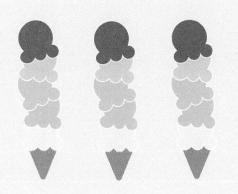

Redeem For

GO OUT FOR ICE CREAM

VALID WHENEVER!

Redeem For

PAJAMAS DAY

VALID ON WEEKENDS & HOLIDAYS

Redeem For

MINUTES OF EXTRA SCREEN TIME

VALID ON WEEKENDS & HOLIDAYS

TO:

FROM:

TO:

FROM:

TO:

FROM:

TO:

FROM:

TO:

FROM:

Redeem For

SKIP CHORES FOR
A DAY

VALID WHENEVER!

Redeem For

MOVIES AT
THE THEATERS
-WITH POPCORN-

VALID ON WEEKENDS & HOLIDAYS

Redeem For

BREAKFAST FOR
DINNER

VALID WHENEVER!

Redeem For

$ TO SPEND
AT A STORE

VALID WHENEVER!

Redeem For

STAY UP   HOUR
PAST BEDTIME

VALID ON WEEKENDS & HOLIDAYS

TO:

FROM:

TO:

FROM:

TO:

FROM:

TO:

FROM:

TO:

FROM:

Redeem For

DINNER AT A RESTAURANT OF YOUR CHOICE

VALID ON WEEKENDS & HOLIDAYS

Redeem For

DATE WITH DAD
YOUR CHOICE OF ACTIVITY

VALID ON WEEKENDS & HOLIDAYS

Redeem For

SKIP A VEGETABLE (OR ITEM OF YOUR CHOICE) FOR ONE MEAL

VALID WHENEVER!

Redeem For

GAME NIGHT
YOUR CHOICE OF GAME

VALID ON WEEKENDS & HOLIDAYS

Redeem For

EXTRA BEDTIME STORY(IES)

VALID WHENEVER!

TO:

FROM:

TO:

FROM:

TO:

FROM:

TO:

FROM:

TO:

FROM:

Redeem For

DATE WITH MOM
YOUR CHOICE OF ACTIVITY

VALID ON WEEKENDS & HOLIDAYS

Redeem For

FAMILY ACTIVITY
OF YOUR CHOICE

VALID ON WEEKENDS & HOLIDAYS

Redeem For

SLEEPOVER AT MOM
AND DAD'S ROOM

VALID ON WEEKENDS & HOLIDAYS

Redeem For

FAMILY
DANCE PARTY

VALID ON WEEKENDS & HOLIDAYS

Redeem For

ONE BREAKFAST
IN BED

VALID ON WEEKENDS & HOLIDAYS

TO:

FROM:

TO:

FROM:

TO:

FROM:

TO:

FROM:

TO:

FROM:

Redeem For

ONE TREAT OF YOUR CHOICE

VALID ON WEEKENDS & HOLIDAYS

Redeem For

HOST A SLEEPOVER

VALID ON WEEKENDS & HOLIDAYS

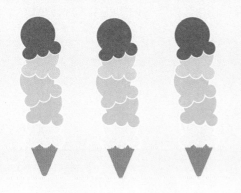

Redeem For

GO OUT FOR ICE CREAM

VALID WHENEVER!

Redeem For

PAJAMAS DAY

VALID ON WEEKENDS & HOLIDAYS

Redeem For

MINUTES OF EXTRA SCREEN TIME

VALID ON WEEKENDS & HOLIDAYS

TO:

FROM:

TO:

FROM:

TO:

FROM:

TO:

FROM:

TO:

FROM:

Redeem For

SKIP CHORES FOR A DAY

VALID WHENEVER!

Redeem For

MOVIES AT THE THEATERS
-WITH POPCORN-

VALID ON WEEKENDS & HOLIDAYS

Redeem For

BREAKFAST FOR DINNER

VALID WHENEVER!

Redeem For

$ TO SPEND AT A STORE

VALID WHENEVER!

Redeem For

STAY UP   HOUR PAST BEDTIME

VALID ON WEEKENDS & HOLIDAYS

TO:

FROM:

TO:

FROM:

TO:

FROM:

TO:

FROM:

TO:

FROM:

Redeem For

DINNER AT A RESTAURANT OF YOUR CHOICE

VALID ON WEEKENDS & HOLIDAYS

Redeem For

DATE WITH DAD
YOUR CHOICE OF ACTIVITY

. VALID ON WEEKENDS & HOLIDAYS

Redeem For

SKIP A VEGETABLE (OR ITEM OF YOUR CHOICE) FOR ONE MEAL

VALID WHENEVER!

Redeem For

GAME NIGHT
YOUR CHOICE OF GAME

VALID ON WEEKENDS & HOLIDAYS

Redeem For

EXTRA BEDTIME STORY(IES)

VALID WHENEVER!

TO:

FROM:

TO:

FROM:

TO:

FROM:

TO:

FROM:

TO:

FROM:

Redeem For

DATE WITH MOM
YOUR CHOICE OF ACTIVITY

VALID ON WEEKENDS & HOLIDAYS

Redeem For

FAMILY ACTIVITY
OF YOUR CHOICE

VALID ON WEEKENDS & HOLIDAYS

Redeem For

SLEEPOVER AT MOM
AND DAD'S ROOM

VALID ON WEEKENDS & HOLIDAYS

Redeem For

FAMILY
DANCE PARTY

VALID ON WEEKENDS & HOLIDAYS

Redeem For

ONE BREAKFAST
IN BED

VALID ON WEEKENDS & HOLIDAYS

TO:

FROM:

TO:

FROM:

TO:

FROM:

TO:

FROM:

TO:

FROM:

Redeem For

Redeem For

VALID

Redeem For

VALID

Redeem For

VALID

Redeem For

VALID

TO:

FROM:

TO:

FROM:

TO:

FROM:

TO:

FROM:

TO:

FROM:

Redeem For

VALID

Redeem For

VALID

Redeem For

VALID

Redeem For

VALID

Redeem For

VALID

TO:

FROM:

TO:

FROM:

TO:

FROM:

TO:

FROM:

TO:

FROM:

Redeem For

VALID

Redeem For

VALID

Redeem For

VALID

Redeem For

VALID

Redeem For

VALID

TO:

FROM:

TO:

FROM:

TO:

FROM:

TO:

FROM:

TO:

FROM:

Redeem For

VALID

Redeem For

VALID

Redeem For

VALID

Redeem For

VALID

Redeem For

VALID

TO:

FROM:

TO:

FROM:

TO:

FROM:

TO:

FROM:

TO:

FROM:

Redeem For

VALID

Redeem For

VALID

Redeem For

VALID

Redeem For

VALID

Redeem For

VALID

TO:

FROM:

TO:

FROM:

TO:

FROM:

TO:

FROM:

TO:

FROM:

Redeem For

VALID

Redeem For

VALID

Redeem For

VALID

Redeem For

VALID

Redeem For

VALID

TO:

FROM:

TO:

FROM:

TO:

FROM:

TO:

FROM:

TO:

FROM:

Redeem For

VALID

Redeem For

VALID

Redeem For

VALID

Redeem For

VALID

Redeem For

VALID

TO:

FROM:

TO:

FROM:

TO:

FROM:

TO:

FROM:

TO:

FROM:

Redeem For

Redeem For

VALID

Redeem For

VALID

Redeem For

VALID

Redeem For

VALID

TO:

FROM:

TO:

FROM:

TO:

FROM:

TO:

FROM:

TO:

FROM: